FLOWERS FOR YOU

FLOWERS FOR YOU

A Special Gift

For Joan

From Laila

Date 12/5/92

**Reflections on the
Beauty of Living**

FLOWERS FOR YOU

LEROY
BROWNLOW

Brownlow Publishing Company, Inc.

Brownlow Gift Books

A Few Hallelujahs for Your Ho-Hums
A Psalm in My Heart
As a Man Thinketh
Better Than Medicine—A Merry Heart
Children Won't Wait
Flowers for Mother
Flowers for You
Flowers of Friendship
Flowers That Never Fade
For Mom With Love
Give Us This Day
Grandpa Was a Preacher
It's a One-derful Life
Jesus Wept
Just Between Friends
Leaves of Gold
Love Is Forever
Making the Most of Life
The Fruit of the Spirit
The Greatest Thing in the World
The Other Wise Man
Thoughts of Gold—Wisdom for Living
Today and Forever
Today Is Mine
University of Hard Knocks

Contents

The Message of Flowers

*I*f God thought it wise to enrich and sweeten our lives by surrounding us with the beauty and fragrance of flowers, we can be perfectly sure that He meant for us to appreciate their messages and learn from them:

- golden daffodils that dance beside the silvery waters,
- a thousand pale primroses that shine like stars in the shadowy grass,
- buttercups that spot the meadows with fire and gold,
- red roses with a richness of color that excels kings' robes and yet so common that even the poorest can enjoy them,
- daisies with golden eyes to see the day.

But in addition to natural flowers, God has also planted within us spiritual "flowers"—these pure and sweet principles that can live and bud and blossom in the heart and lives of us all.

These nobler principles which enhance the idealism and beauty of our character were so complete and perfect in the life of Christ that flowers were used to describe Him. He is spoken of in the Bible as "the rose of Sharon, and the lily of the valleys" (Song of Solomon 2:1).

May we together strive to keep our hearts a rich and beautiful garden in which the following principles may thrive as fragrant and lovely flowers.

LEROY BROWNLOW

Flower of Faith

Have you ever climbed to the top of a high mountain? If so, you had the experience of cautiously and laboriously going up and down hills, over rocks, around obstructions and across streams. Sometimes it was easy. Sometimes it was hard. But it was always toilsome. From beginning to end, it was a challenge. The thing that pushed your steps onward and upward was faith; you believed you could do it. Without this faith, discouragement would have beckoned you to the lower levels.

Such is true of the road to success in life. At times the going is easy while at other times the uphill struggle is extremely strenuous. No one succeeds by quitting. No one wins by giving up. But to keep moving aright requires faith— as the Bible says, the "faith which worketh by love" (Galatians 5:6).

• *We need faith in God, in self and in others.* This gives us the heroic quality that is unconquerable. This is the stuff that makes men and women, supports communities and builds nations.

This three-fold faith has always been the unbeaten force. Through the ages it has been the never-failing source of man's strength in time of trouble. As the Founding Fathers turned their backs upon the Old World and set sail for the New, it was faith which drove them onward. As they waded ashore to tackle an uncivilized wilderness, their only sustaining power was faith.

Faith gave them strength when their feet faltered.
Faith gave them courage when their hearts sank.
Faith gave them unity when their opinions divided them.

How fitting it was that the sons and daughters of those hearty pioneers should engrave on their money this tribute of faith in the Infinite, "In God we trust."

Don't lose Courage! Spirit brave
Carry with you to the grave.
Don't lose Time in vain distress!
Work, not worry, brings success.
Don't lose Hope! who lets her stray
Goes forlornly all the way.
Don't lose Patience, some what will!
Patience ofttimes outruns skill.
Don't lose Gladness! every hour
Blooms for you some happy flower.
Though be foiled your dearest plan,
Don't lose Faith in God and man!

While atheistic influences are attempting to brainwash our people into believing that it is smart to be a disbeliever, it is wise to remember that one can be an infidel without believing anything, doing anything, or being anything. There is no accomplishment in that.

• *We believe in God because He is the only reasonable explanation of creation and life.* We have to start with something. Either some living being or some dead matter had to be self-existent from which everything else has come. This is conclusive from the following syllogism:

1) Something cannot come from nothing.

2) But something is (does exist).

3) Therefore, something always was.

That self-existent power from which creation originated is God, the eternal Spirit. We admit that, it is hard for human beings with finite and limited understanding to comprehend and fathom the self-existence and the unlimited scope of God. This is to be expected because we are man and not God. We do understand, however, that it is much more plausible to accept God rather than cold, dead matter as the self-existent First Cause. In fact, it is preposterous to say that the First Cause was cold, lifeless matter.

The atheist— not believing in God— is forced to say that a tiny speck of matter was the "first cause" and that the world originated from it; because something had to be self-made. Next, he must get that lifeless speck to be alive; for life can only come from life. If he had all this, he would have something superhuman and divine.

Whether we wish to or not, we are compelled to begin with some self-existent, almighty and eternal power as the First Cause, the Creator. Thus the Bible begins with this introductory thought and starting point: "In the beginning God created the heaven and the earth" (Genesis 1:1). This makes sense. Nothing else does.

The disbeliever's plight is similar to that of the crated dog in the Railway Express office. A gentleman said, "Where is that dog going?" The manager, thoroughly disgusted, said, "I don't know. You don't know. He don't know. Nobody don't know! Because he has already gone and chewed up his tag." The atheist has "chewed up" his tag. He does not know from whence he came, why he is here, or where he is going. This is frustrating. We need to learn that an effective remedy for frustration and tattered nerves is a strong faith in God. This gives meaning and direction to our living.

• *We believe in God because the universe is a big billboard which spells G-O-D.* Everywhere we look there is evidence of divine power. This fact is aptly stated in Psalm 19:1,2: "The heavens declare the glory of God; and the firmament showeth his handiwork. Day unto day uttereth speech, and night unto night showeth knowledge.'" Our own feeble understanding assures us this is right.

Scientists daily discover countless numbers of planets and stars we have never been able to see. The immensity of space goes on and on. Remember that if you have trouble fathoming

God, you also have trouble fathoming space. Though we do not fully comprehend either, we believe in both. We ask: what power brought all this space and all these stars into existence? If God did not, who or what did?

To answer the question by contending that all these heavenly bodies are an accident is just as silly as to argue that your local telephone directory is the result of an explosion in a printing shop. There are far more stars hanging in space than there are letters in the telephone directory, and they are just as much in order.

An infidel once said to a French peasant: "We will tear down your churches. We will destroy everything that reminds you of God." The humble peasant replied, "But you will leave us the sun, the moon, and the stars; and as long as they shine, we shall have a reminder of God."

• *The fact that there can be no law without a lawgiver proves there must be a Supreme Lawmaker.* There are many laws in nature, and the law of gravitation will serve as an example. Gravitation is a force which moves our earth rapidly, systematically and orderly so that the seasons and the days come in regular order. This same force makes all the planets move in perfect precision, so much so that astronomers can correctly predict an eclipse a hundred years from now.

The law of gravitation is so dependable that when we go to bed at night we never wonder if the sun will come up at the right time. Inasmuch as there can be no law without a lawmaker, then who made the law of gravitation? It must be the work of the Divine Being. It is kept in operation by the power of His word, as the Bible explains: "But the heavens and the earth, which are now, by the same word are kept in store" (II Peter 3:7).

• *The universality of man's religious nature bears witness to the existence of God.* No nation or tribe of people has ever been discovered that does not believe in some kind of Supreme Being. All of them without exception practice some form of religion. It is true that many of the religions are heathen and false; but the fact that all religions have resemblances proves that they came from a common source, and that source a pure one which is God. The explanation of the corruptions of God's true revelation to man is found in the Bible: "God hath made man upright, but they have sought out many inventions" (Ecclesiastes 7:9).

The prevalence of man's religious nature proves that he is different from the animals, that he has a spirit, being the offspring of the Great Spirit. This fact which is so obvious to all of us is, of course, mentioned in the Bible: "That they should seek the Lord, if haply they might feel after him, and find him, though he be not far from every one of us: For in him we live, and move, and have our being; as certain of your own poets have said, For we are also his offspring" (Acts 17:26-28).

• *We can and do believe in the God we cannot see with the material eye.* Yet the atheist says, "I cannot see God, and I won't believe in a thing I cannot see." A disbeliever was asked if there is a God. He replied, "I don't know. I have never seen one."

The same illogical reasoning would have forced him to rule out many of the known qualities of life. For instance, electricity cannot be seen. You cannot tell by looking which wire is cold and which is hot. While electricity is not visible, the fruits and evidences are easily observed. When you see a person sorrowing, you do not see the sorrow but rather the evidences of it. Neither is pain visible. A suffering man says to the dentist, "This tooth is killing me." Suppose the doctor, after the examination, should say, "You have no pain because I cannot see it." No one would be so foolish. Then why should one make the same ridiculous argument against the existence of God?

God is a spirit and thus cannot be seen with the eye of flesh, but this does not prove that He is unreal. There is abundant evidence that God does exist and that He is here.

• *We can and do believe in a Power we are unable to fully comprehend.* The disbeliever says, "I cannot understand the self-existence, the everlasting nature, and the almighty power of God." He then adds, "I won't believe anything I cannot explain." Of course, he does. As an atheist, he has no explanation for the origin of the world, but he does believe it exists. Neither does he have an explanation for the conscious life of man— why man has a conscience and the animals do not— but he believes it.

Our finite minds certainly cannot fully comprehend the infinite God, because we are not God. He is too big for our understanding, but we can and do believe that He exists.

Flower of Assurance

A strong faith in God fills our heart with assurance. Through faith we have learned to trust in him rather than ourselves. Solomon said: "Trust in the Lord with all thine heart; and lean not unto thine own understanding" (Proverbs 3:5). This assurance is our sustaining strength as we face every eventuality of life. It dries our tears, heals our broken hearts, strengthens our hands and gives direction to our feet.

• *We have the assurance that God will give us strength to equal our needs.* We have come to know the real meaning of this heartening promise expressed in the Bible: "As thy days, so shall thy strength be" (Deuteronomy 33:25). This is why that when we have often become dead tired in life's journey and felt the temptation to drop in our tracks, we found an added strength that enabled us to triumph over adversity.

• *We have the assurance that God will blot out our sins, if we trust Him and obey His gospel.* This confidence gives us tranquility and peace of heart. The frustrations and nervous disorders of

many people are often due to their guilt feelings. It is easy for this emotional disturbance to grip any of us; "for all have sinned, and have come short of the glory of God" (Romans 3:23).

Everybody wants peace, but not everybody knows how to find it. Some have tried to soothe a biting conscience by refusing to admit any guilt. But they are not deceiving anyone, not even themselves. They need pardon, despite their refusal to seek it. Others, having feelings of guilt, have tried to find relief through the infraction of more moral standards and divine rules. Distressed souls, however, have never found inward harmony by adding sin to sin. This merely aggravates the disturbance.

The only practical solution is the one laid down in the Bible: get forgiveness. God has promised: "Though your sins be as scarlet, they shall be as white as snow; though they be red like crimson, they shall be as wool" (Isaiah 1:18). And God has further promised: "For I will be merciful to their unrighteousness, and their sins and their iniquities will I remember no more" (Hebrews 8:12). When God forgives sin, He does not bring it up again. If God is willing to let sin, when forgiven, remain in the past, then so should we.

There is enough sin in every one's past to haunt him, if he dwells upon it. This was true of even the great Apostle Paul who wrote much of the New Testament. He declared that he was once the chief of sinners. Yet he obtained mercy; God forgave him; and, forgetting the things which were behind, Paul reached forth unto those things which were before (Philippians 3:13,14). This is the only practical and peaceful way to live— a life of faith.

You can actually know that your sins are forgiven and that everything is well with you. You do not have to guess about it. You have God's word for it. This is the blessed assurance He has given us: "And hereby we do know that we know him, if we keep his commandments" (I John 2:3).

One of man's sweetest and most precious thoughts is God's eagerness to forgive. This is portrayed in the merciful story of the Prodigal Son (Luke 15).

We are reminded of a modern day prodigal who sinned against his father and left home. Through the years he did not let his family know where he was. The passing of time, however, did not heal his longing to return home. Finally he wrote a letter to his father in which he stated that he was sorry, begged for pardon, and related his desire to go home. But he mentioned that he had no assurance his father would receive him. The railroad tracks ran at the back of their farm. There was a pecan tree not far from where the trains passed. He stated in the letter that he would be on the train a certain day. He asked the father to put a white cloth on the pecan tree if he would forgive him and receive him, and stated that if he saw it was there, he would get off at the next stop and return home. As the train rounded the bend and came up the grade, this prodigal son's heart pounded with anxiety. Would the white cloth be there? He strained his eyes for a glimpse of hope. As he got closer he saw a sight to behold— a white cloth on every limb.

This illustrates in a feeble way the forgiving nature of God. If you have sin in your life, get forgiveness; and then forget it, so far as guilt is concerned.

The Father's forgiveness, each time sin is pardoned, enables us to enter each time anew the land of beginning again.

The Land of Beginning Again

I wish there were some wonderful place
Called the land of beginning again,
Where all our mistakes and all our heartaches,
And all our selfish grief,
Could be dropped like a shabby coat at the door
And never put on again.

That land is a reality. That land is ours by the grace of God.

• *Aware of the Almighty power and loving kindness of God, our faith in Him gives us assurance to face even death.* The apostle Paul said, "I know whom I have believed" (II Timothy 1:12). Faith was the basis of his philosophy of life and death, stated as follows: "For to me to live is Christ, and to die is gain" (Philippians 1:21). So in giving his farewell message at the end of life's journey, we hear his words ring with calm assurance and eternal hope:

For I am now ready to be offered, and the time of my departure is at hand.

I have fought a good fight, I have finished my course, I have kept the faith:

Henceforth there is laid up for me a crown of righteousness, which the Lord, the righteous judge, shall give me at that day: and not to me only, but unto all them also that love his appearing.

II TIMOTHY 4:6-8

Death was only a few paces ahead, but Paul was unafraid. Faith had dispelled fear. He did not know all about death and all about what is on eternity's shore, but he knew his Lord was there and that was enough.

A few years ago a physician visited a dying patient. The good doctor was a man of faith. The sick man was frightened and wanted to know about death and eternity. The doctor tenderly and sympathetically answered these questions from the Bible. The he opened the door to leave, and at that moment his dog sprang into the room. The physician turned and said: "This is my dog. He did not know what was on the other side of the door, except that his master was there. But that was assurance enough for him; so when the door was cracked he passed through." He then added: "That is the way I feel. I do not know all about what is on the other side, but I do know my Master is there and that is enough; so when the door is opened I shall pass through with confidence."

Years ago I visited the celebrated park in St. Louis. There were towering trees, green grass, beautiful flowers, fragrant roses and singing birds everywhere. In one section there was a memorial to the Korean War dead. As we approached the memorial, constructed in the hallowed memory of those who had given life for country, I saw the stars and stripes, the red, white and blue, waving in the gentle breezes. The enrapturing melody of the chimes rang forth in the background. At the base of the flag pole there was a large clock some thirty feet in diameter and raised about a foot and a half above the ground. On the face of the clock there were lovely flowers growing between the numbers. At the foot of the clock in the midst of a beautiful arrangement of flowers were these raised word: "Hours and Flowers Soon Fade Away." Time cuts down and destroys everything that is material. Only that which is eternal can survive time. After hours have passed and flowers have wilted, the immortal soul still remains. The hope of immortality is too necessary not to be true. The Bible says, "Then shall the dust return to the earth as it was: and the spirit shall return to God who gave it" (Ecclesiastes 12:7).

In the Tate Gallery in London is one of the last and most famous paintings of Frederic Watts. A shrouded form lies upon a bier in the middle of the room. On a table nearby is an open book, and against the table leans a voiceless lyre. In one corner of the room is the colorful mantle of a nobleman and in the other corner a lance and shield and several pieces of armor, with roses strewn over them to show that the arts of life were mingled with the sterner duties of the world. But now all is over. All is quiet. The still and lifeless form cannot read the book nor seize the lance, nor touch the lyre, nor don the mantle, nor catch the fragrance of the roses. All is over. On the wall in the background are three statements:

What I spent I had.
What I saved I lost.
What I gave I have.

It is through faith we are confident that whatever we have given in time, enthusiasm, labors and tears to the strengthening of man's inner nature— that and that alone is our and ours forever. Everything else fades.

It is this faith in God that generates faith in self and others. This three-fold faith dries the tears of sorrow, heals the hearts of mourning, strengthens the hands that falter and gives meaning to life that is fleeting.

Faith gives choice to the nobler ideals, and following them, we reach our destiny.

Flower of Happiness

The flower of happiness is most unusual, even though all people desire it. Surface and momentary delights are easily found because they have a thousand sources; but they are all fleeting. Time takes them away. The fun of youth and the enjoyment of health, the joys of success and the gratification of recognition are perpetually passing away. The joy of each is exhausted by its consumption. Our hearts cry out, therefore, for a joy that is more satisfying and lasting.

• *Our desire for happiness is a natural one.* It is a law of nature that every living being or thing seeks a better and fuller life in keeping with the environment. It is natural for the flower to bloom. It is in accordance with nature for the sap in the tree to flow toward foliage and fruit. It is natural for the little bird's blood to beat toward song and flight. Now in man, a conscious being, this upward swing takes a conscious movement, which is happiness— the harmony of the inward life, the music of the heart. This desire is inborn in the heart of every being. Our

souls reach for something that satisfies.

• *We are the greatest obstacle to our own happiness.* We are apt to lay the blame on others or on circumstances. We shrink from accusing self. Friends may counsel and encourage, but in the long run it is something we will have to achieve for ourselves.

For happiness to grow in the heart there must be an understanding and resolution relative to the principles which cause it to sprout and live, bud and blossom. Hence, we offer some suggestions:

• *A program of self-improvement is the first step in acquiring happiness.* Undoubtedly people are born with different dispositions affecting their cheerfulness or gloom. Also, the early influences of life tell upon us. Some parents surround their children with an environment of unrest and tension, bitterness and discontent. Others make for them an atmosphere of freedom and relaxation, love and joy. Unquestionably, in spite of birth or rearing, the most deep-seated tendency to anxiety and gloom can be overcome and replaced with peace and happiness. It takes decision. It takes resolution. It takes courage. It takes persistence. But it can be done.

One of the greatest characters in the Bible said, "I can do all things through Christ which strengtheneth me" (Philippians 4:13). Happiness stems from a fruitful life. Begin today to make yourself sweeter and nobler in heart and more helpful to mankind. Keep on. Never give up. It takes time to acquire any of the arts, and the greatest of all is the art of living.

• *Once-for-all decisions to do right make for happiness.* There can be no peace of mind when one is pulled between conflicting choices. We cannot have our cake and eat it, too. We obtain one desire at the price of giving up another. We need to decide which is more important. The person who vacillates in this decision between honesty and dishonesty becomes greatly frustrated, and this is true of all other moral and religious decisions. On the other hand, the person who makes a once-for-all decision to do right is neither vexed with indecision nor tormented with wrong decision.

A few years ago an earnest and cheerful man said, "I decide at the beginning of every year whether I am going to the best of my ability to attend church every Sunday of the year. I could not stand the strain of deciding the matter every week. I fear it would result in a nervous breakdown before the year is out."

There is a wonderful and helpful truth in this semi-humorous confession. There is a great waste of time, nervous energy and will power in having to decide every day matters of duty and right that should have been decided once for all a long time ago. There is a gratifying amount of internal peace and happiness in having your mind made up to do right and in doing it.

Sow a thought, you reap an act;
Sow an act, you reap a habit;
Sow a habit, you reap a character;
Sow a character, you reap a destiny.

• *Happiness makes happiness.* A woman was left a widow with several children on a little farm at the edge of town. She had many sorrows and heavy burdens to bear. Her responsibilities of rearing the children and making a living were great.

The remarkable thing is that this woman was known for her cheerful and happy spirit. Her comment was: "You know I have no surplus money. I have nothing to give but myself, my words and my deeds; so I resolved that I would do that as best I can. We have five cows and sell the milk from four of them; but I give the milk from the other one to people in much worse condition than ourselves. We call her the sunshine cow because she makes our lives brighter. I have tried to face my troubles bravely and to smile in the face of misfortune. I make it a policy always to speak a happy word to everyone who comes into my presence."

This widow was happy in her unselfish works and by them created a sunny home for her fatherless children. The more we divide our happiness the more we have left.

• *Our acceptance of self gives us peace.* The above-mentioned widow accepted her state and worked from there. She could have made herself miserable and cast a cloud of gloom over her children by bemoaning her life and by refusing to accept it. Our own attitude is more important than the circumstances.

> *One ship drives East and another drives West*
> *With the selfsame winds that blow,*
> *'Tis the set of the sails and not the gales*
> *Which tell us the way to go.*
>
> — ELLA WHEELER WILCOX

When we honestly accept ourselves as we are, we find it not only calming to the nerves but also a realistic step toward improvement. Yes, there are different gifts and talents. The Bible says, "All members have not he same office" (Romans 12:4,5).

If our goal is entirely out of proportion to our ability, then we need to change our goal; otherwise our life will be wrecked with disappointments. A goal should be reachable. For instance, if we cannot be a teacher, we can be a student and this is elevating. If we cannot fill the pulpit, we can fill the pew.

Not only must we accept our ability, but also our stature, the color of our eyes and complexion, disfigurements and abnormalities if they exist. The world is willing to accept us provided we are willing to accept ourselves. It accepted Fanny J. Crosby. She became blind at six weeks of age. Today worship services the world over ring with the sweet and touching hymns she wrote. It accepted Franklin D. Roosevelt. Polio consigned him to a wheel chair, but the American people placed him in the Presidential Chair longer than any other man.

These examples tell us that our handicaps, when accepted, can be turned into stepping-stones.

• *It takes faith to have a happy life.* A great man of faith once said, "I know whom I have believed, and am persuaded that he is able to keep that which I have committed unto him against that day" (II Timothy 1:12).

The person of faith will fret never, but trust ever; will love and labor, sympathize and serve; will never doubt a future God can see or stagger at a promise of help God has given. He believes that "all things work together for good to them that love God" (Romans 8:28). There are so many things we do not now understand and never will in this life; but it adds to our happiness to accept them by faith.

• *Happiness comes from giving ourselves to a cause bigger than ourselves.* The Bible reads, "Happy is that people whose God is the Lord" (Psalm 144:15). The giving of self brings the sweetest peace and the brightest happiness.

The happiest person we have ever known had what most people would consider cause for a bleeding heart and a nerve-racking existence. When she became a Christian, it so upset her husband that he literally kicked her out and told her not to return. She had to work for a living. This woman's faith grew and as it grew her usefulness grew; and as both grew, her happiness increased. She taught a Bible class of boys and girls. Never before or since have we seen a teacher so loved and appreciated by her students. She was their light in darkness and their comfort in trouble. They sat with her at church. She took them home with her for Sunday dinner. They walked by her side and held her hands. She found peace in giving herself to the molding of their lives. She has long since passed across the river of death, but her deeds continue to live.

• *Christ gave us the beatitudes for our happiness.* Christ's rules point to the need of man's first changing himself rather than external circumstances. This is where the multitudes err in their search for happiness— they look without instead of within. It is not to be found in positions, but in dispositions. It is not what you have but what has you that determines it. Misinformed reformers vainly try to construct happy lives and communities out of selfish, unforgiving, vindictive, proud, hardened, and unmerciful persons. It cannot be done. Their plan only calls for a clean-up of outward conditions. Their first cry is: get your circumstances changed. Christ's first cry is: change yourself, and then the things around you will change.

Jesus a long time before psychologists and psychiatrists ever devised rules for mental health said in Matthew 5:1-12:

1) "Blessed [happy] are the poor in spirit"— those who have a sense of spiritual bankruptcy. We must empty ourselves before God can fill us. This virtue is the opposite of pride. We have never seen a happy proud person. It is too easy for his pride to be upset, ever to be happy.

2) "Blessed [happy] are they that mourn"— that is, those who mourn because of sins. The hardened, cynical person only builds up more misery in his heart. On the other hand, the person who is touched by his mistakes seeks pardon from God and man; he can say, "I was wrong; I am sorry; forgive me." This is the happy soul. Of such people, Jesus said, "For they shall be comforted." Even though it seems paradoxical, God will turn the sorrow into joy, just like He makes the rainbow out of a storm and the most beautiful sunset where there are clouds.

3) "Blessed [happy] are the meek"— those who are patient, forgiving, submissive to wrong instead of retaliatory; and who accept God's dealings as absolutely good and wise, without

murmur or resistance.

4) "Blessed [happy] are they which do hunger and thirst after righteousness"— those who have an appetite for a higher degree of righteous living. This hunger has the largest and sweetest satisfaction. This beatitude gives us an ideal to live up to and an achievement to die with. Inner peace comes from a commitment to higher principles and an attainment in self-respect.

5) "Blessed [happy] are the merciful"— those who are forgiving of the wrongs of others and who are helpful in relieving the miseries of unfortunate mankind They will receive mercy from both God and their fellowmen in return. Society in most cases has a way of giving us back the very attitude we have manifested toward it. We have seen many warm-hearted, cheerful, lovable people; and without an exception each one was merciful.

6) "Blessed [happy] are the pure in heart"— those who are free from evil desires and purposes. The scheming, conniving, impure soul can only live a degraded and unhappy existence; and the lower he sinks, the more frantic and frustrated he becomes. The search for peace becomes a futile one in a world of happiness-mirages, which at a distance look good but when touched, tasted and handled can offer nothing more than a temporary "kick" instead of lasting joy.

7) "Blessed [happy] are the peacemakers"— those who promote peace. There is no joy in strife. Happiness is found in peace and in following a course which produces it. The peace-

makers "shall be called the children of God," because they are like Him who sent His Son to the world to secure "peace on earth and good will among men."

8) "Blessed [happy] are they which are persecuted for righteousness' sake"— those who nobly and bravely stand up in the midst of persecution, continuing their righteous deeds even though they are offensive to their persecutors. The person who does this has a conviction and the character to support it in the face of trials. No wonder he is happy. This is the reason the early Christians could rejoice in persecution. The more they suffered, the stronger they became.

It is evident from the beatitudes that happiness comes from giving up self with all of its cheap and shoddy traits to find one's self again in a sweeter and nobler character.

For this is peace,— to lose the lonely note
Of self in love's celestial-ordered strain;
And this is joy,— to find one's self again
In him whose harmonies forever float
Through all the spheres of song, below, above,—
For God is music, even as God is love.

Flower of Contentment

We once reflected upon the differences of a boy and a dog as they played. The boy was six and the dog was seven. The dog ran on four legs, the boy on two; yet a short time ago the boy was using his hands and going about on all fours. But time made a difference. Something in the boy made him a citizen of a higher world. That something had a marked effect upon their lives.

Both were busy digging. The dog dug up the bone he had buried the day before, carried it over into the sunshine, and there he lay, gnawing it and occasionally growling over it in fun. He was blissfully contented. Sunshine, quiet and a bone— that was all he needed.

The boy was building a house and was in the process of digging the basement. Of course, he did not build a house of much size or stability. But this is only a secondary thought.

The point is that the boy had an idea of a completed house and the dog did not, even though he was a year older. Nor

would the dog ever have an idea of such a elaborate dream if he should live to be a thousand. The dog was satisfied with things as they are, just so long as the sun shone and a bigger dog did not try to take that bone from him. But it was different with the boy. He worked to improve conditions. He pondered matters and weighed one thing against another. It is this desire to change, to make, to improve, to build, which is the dynamic power of all progress.

These powerful impulses are wonderful, but they must be controlled by faith, trust and common sense, or else our days will be wrecked with fretfulness and worry. Our beautiful and glorious nature should not be abused and used against us. We can plan and make progress and still have contentment— because peace of heart comes from within.

• *Even though we were designed for progress, we can have contentment in any state.* One of the world's most persecuted men said in the Bible, "I have learned, in whatsoever state I am, therewith to be content" (Philippians 4:11). He did not say that he had no desire to improve his lot— this would be contrary to man's nature. He said that he had learned peace of mind. This lesson saved him from the waste of energy through worry and fretfulness. He had peace because he was at peace with himself.

Contentment can be found in what the world considers unlikely places, such as poverty, misfortune, sorrow, disappointment and pain. We can find it there if we will but look. Struggle is often a blessing in disguise.

Recently the newspapers carried the story of some sea-gulls literally starving to death. For generation after generation the birds had lived on the scraps thrown out by a fish cannery. Then when it closed down, the seagulls were helpless. They had lost their ability to seek out their food and care for themselves. What was once thought to be a great blessing for them turned out to be a tragedy.

God knew what was best for us in arranging life with its trials and challenges.

Regardless of circumstances, we should search for peace of mind where we are, even though it be in the commonplace realms, the humdrum ways of life, the tame and sober duties, or in the linings of the dark clouds which hover over us. Those humble duties, when honorably discharged, are filled with joy and contentment and those storm-clouds we feared have silver linings. It may amaze you to learn that you can discover a dowry of peace and strength even in the ministry of pain. While the physical man suffers, there can be a compensation for it by the inward man's discovery of a trust, a sympathy and a hope not to be found in surface living.

Life's shadows which all of us sooner or later must pass through may give rest to eyes which have become tired and bored with too much sunlight. Too much of life's sunlight blinds us to realities. After passing through the shadows we can see better than ever. Life's overcast sky frequently "restoreth the soul."

The clouds ye so much dread
Are big with mercy, and shall break
In blessing on your head.

• *Living life a day at a time brings contentment.* This keeps us from borrowing trouble. Christ said in the Sermon on the Mount: "Take therefore no thought for the morrow: for the morrow shall take thought for the things of itself. Sufficient unto the day is the evil thereof" (Matthew 6:33). The passage does not teach against plans for tomorrow. It teaches that we should take care of life's duties day by day, free of anxiety. After all, this is the best preparation we can make for the future. Many of our problems are due to our failure to take care of the day-before duties. Each day brings trouble enough for itself without worrying about tomorrow's problems, the most of which perhaps will never come. True, there will be some adversities tomorrow. This world is not heaven. But God will give us sufficient grace to bear the trouble when it comes. We have not the strength to bear trouble three times: before it comes, when it comes, and after it comes. By facing only the adversities that do arise, it will save us from a thousand imaginary ones that never become real.

After Abraham Lincoln was elected to the Presidency, he was interviewed relative to the impending Civil War. He replied: "I am much like the old preacher in a crowded coach nearing a swollen river. He had listened in silence to the tedious expressions of anxiety respecting the perilous fording of the

stream till the passengers, somewhat vexed at his seeming indif-
ference, asked his opinion. He replied, 'I make it a practice
never to cross a river till I get to it.'"

As time goes on, we learn that the rivers are not too hard to
cross and in many instances are rolling with refreshing and
friendly waters, and that the lions along the way are generally
chained and quite often are only stuffed or carved figures.

• *The habit of worry needs to be overcome and replaced with
confidence.* The habit becomes so routine with many people that
they even worry about things they forget to worry about. A
friend who suddenly became visibly depressed a few years ago
explained his feelings by saying, "I am worrying about something and cannot seem to remember what it is." He had not forgotten his worry; he was worrying all the more because he had
forgotten its cause.

• *It calms our nerves to know that success can come out of failure.*
This is seen in a fish story in the Bible. Peter said, "Master, we
have toiled all the night, and have taken nothing; nevertheless
at Thy word, I will let down the net" (Luke 5:5).

No doubt, it was the same old story: the fish were not running; or the wind was in the wrong direction; or the water was
too muddy. Anyway they had caught nothing— failure.
However, when they took Jesus' advice, "Launch out into the
deep, and let down your nets for a drought," they caught more
than the net would hold— success. At first Peter was a little
reluctant to do this because he was an experienced fisherman
and his opinion ruled it out; but when he threw the responsibili-

ty of success entirely upon the shoulders of the Lord, he found true success. In failure he learned to put more trust in the Lord and less trust in self. He had to fail before he could succeed. Failure always has a victorious effect upon us when it leads us to do what Jesus commands, regardless of apparent reasons to the contrary. When we pursue this course and depend upon it, there will never be real failure.

Of course, Peter still had to do what he could for himself. Christ's plan called for Peter to launch out and cast the net and pull it in. Some people fail because they expect the Lord to do everything, while others fail because they expect Him to do nothing. God gives us the directions, but we have to follow them; figuratively, He tells us where the fish are, but we have to throw the net.

Life is filled with success followed by failure and failure followed by success. We have seen it happen so many times. It can happen to you. Cheer up.

• *A true view of life is needed to have contentment.* Much of our discontent can be traced to our false view of the ends of living. Some people are under the spell that leisure and fun are the only purposes of living. The result is they are not prepared for the sterner calls of duty.

As an example, a sailor boy joins the navy. A few weeks later he slips over the side of his ship and flees as a deserter. Why? He had a false ideal of a sailor's life. He had it pictured that he would have nothing to do but to smoothly sail, sail in a sea of glass until he landed in some faraway tropical port. He would have nothing to do but dress in a glamorous uniform and spend his time beneath a full moon, courting some dark-eyed beauty of the Orient, amidst all the luxury of the East. But it turned out differently. They put him to scrubbing decks and washing dishes. A false ideal was too much for him.

Now do not laugh at him; for his mistake is society's mistake. This is why the cloud of gloom hovers over so many. Their expectations are out of harmony with realities.

• *We can increase our contentment by counting our blessings.* We can say that every good gift is from God and "that he did good, and gave us rain from heaven, and fruitful seasons, filling our hearts with food and gladness" (James 1:17; Acts 14:17). Ingratitude is a product of selfishness, and misery is the fruit of both. Many people make themselves content by counting their blessings, while others make themselves unhappy by harping on the things they do not have. We can make ourselves rich by decreasing our wants.

> *When upon life's billows you are tempest-tossed,*
> *When you are discouraged, thinking all is lost,*
> *Count your many blessings, name them one by one,*
> *And it will surprise you what the Lord hath done.*
> — JOHNSON OATMAN

A lady related this story: As a cold rain beat down, a little boy and girl knocked at her door. Her first impulse was to tell them to go away. She was cleaning house and cooking roast beef, brown potatoes and tasty gravy for the evening meal. But one look at their damp feet and sad eyes changed this as they said, "Lady, you got any old papers?"

"My, my, you children must be soaked; come in; you are cold; stand over by the fire."

She went to get the papers but her mind was not on papers. She thought of food to fortify those little bodies against the wintry chill. After bringing the papers she said, "When I was a little girl I especially liked bread and jam and hot chocolate. I'll bring you some."

"Oh, no lady, we only wanted the papers, something you would not use any way."

"Never mind that," this woman with a heart said. "I'll be back in a jiffy." And she was, and with curious, wide-open eyes the children gazed at this and that as they ate. She then went back to the kitchen to test the dinner she was cooking. When she returned to the living room the little girl held up the cup and saucer and said, "Lady, are you rich?"

"Oh, my, no, why do you ask?"

"Your cups match your saucers," was the reply.

They were inexpensive as was the house and everything in it. Shortly the children took their papers and stepped out to face the cold winds, winds from the North and from another viewpoint, the winds of opposition. Then the good lady thought of her blessings, so many things that matched: roast and brown gravy, bread and potatoes, a house and furniture, a good husband with a job.

At this point as she tidied up the room, her eyes fell upon

the little footprints left upon the hearth; but she left them, telling herself, "I want to leave them, so if I should ever be tempted to forget how rich I really am, I can look at those little prints and remember what they have taught me."

• *The greatest single contributing factor to contentment is faith and trust in God.* Apprehension possesses us because we doubt our beliefs and believe our doubts. Our nerves crack because our faith has already broken. Let us read our Bible for more faith. "Faith cometh by hearing, and hearing by the word of God" (Romans 10:17).

We need the faith to accept trustingly the promise: "My God shall supply all your need" (Philippians 4:19). "All" is a big word, but God is big enough to do it.

Flower of Optimism

No more charming and sweet-scented flower ever grew in human hearts than optimism. As it blooms, there falls from it some of the necessary seeds of success. Surely there can be no substitute for brains; but if there could be, optimism would no doubt be it. The most brilliant plans produced by the most competent minds never amount to anything when smothered with pessimism.

Shakespeare said:

Our doubts are traitors
And make us lose the good we oft might win,
By fearing to attempt.

If we would be successful and happy, we must cultivate the flower of optimism and it will put us on the sunny side of life. But in contrast, the pessimist makes himself miserable by imagining the worst is going to happen. This was true of the man who said, "When I feel good, I always feel bad; because I know

that I am going to feel worse later." A victim of his own fears.

Yet we know that the most faithful and pious souls must occasionally fight the moods of depression. There are times, at least momentarily, when the most optimistic and visionary persons have difficulty seeing the bright side of life. There are reasons for it, but there are also good reasons for optimism in our over-all view of life. As we now ponder a few of them, we expect our flower of optimism to grow and bloom a little fuller.

• *It is easier to be optimistic when one is enjoying health and is free of physical pain.* Even though one's soul is prospering, his body may be afflicted with wretched health. This thought was on John's heart as he wrote Gaius: "Beloved, I wish above all things that thou mayest prosper and be in health, even as thy soul prospereth" (III John 2).

There are many examples of despondency that are born of physical pain. One of the classic examples is in the life of Job who said, "Oh that I might have my request. . . even that it would please God to destroy me" (Job 6:8,9). His outlook was temporarily dimmed by suffering. But it is heart-warming to note that this man who was tried and tested to the limits— loss of children, health, finances, and his wife's encouragement— later found strength to endure and thus said, "Though he slay me, yet will I trust in him" (Job 13:15). A remarkable change had occurred: not in Job's afflictions, but in his own heart which enabled him to bear his suffering.

• *Association with optimistic friends will help to keep fear and despondency away.* The Bible says, "Know ye not that a little leaven leaveneth the whole lump?" (I Corinthians 5:6). It works this way for good or bad, for optimism or pessimism. If you greet your neighbor with a smile, he is apt to smile; but with a frown, he is apt to return it. Like begets like. Influence is powerful.

If you were ever confined to your bed for a long time with illness, perhaps you had both optimists and pessimists to visit you. You know which you preferred. When the radiant optimist walked into the room and spoke words of faith and hope, it seemed that the whole room lighted up with cheer. You who had secretly suffered sinking spells of pessimism regained your confidence and began to view your problems with renewed optimism. But the gloomy person's visit had the opposite effect. When he entered, it seemed that a shadow had fallen across the room. His conversation was based on failure, doubt and fear.

He borders his spirit with black
And hangs his hope with crepe.
He can't enjoy the sun today—
It may rain tomorrow.
When a pain won't come his way,
Future pains he borrows.
If there is good news to be heard,
He stuffs his ears with cotton,
Evils dire are oft inferred,
Good is all forgotten.

Mental habits have contributed to the pessimism of many people. They have the habit of being pessimistic. They cultivated it; and to keep it growing, they usually find someone of like disposition to whom they may talk or write and each tries to excel the other in singing a song of woe.

If we would cultivate the bright view of life, we will find help from the associations of those who hope for the best. It is much easier to be optimistic when hopeful friends are near. In the evening when danger seems most imminent and fears are the greatest, people of common interests find strength in huddling together like frightened sheep in a storm. The persecuted disciples of Jesus did this (John 20:19). It worked for them and it will for us.

There is strength to be obtained by joining hands with the courageous, by belonging to a group— the church, a Bible class, etc.— by having mutual interests which bind your heart to the hearts of the brave and optimistic. Many people who were in the beginning process of developing the habit of gloom have been pulled back from this negative thinking and encouraged to think positively by these wonderful heart-ties.

• *Faith is a key to optimism.* We need faith in God and faith in ourselves. Pessimism cannot dwell in the heart where there is strong, unconquerable faith. It has been said, "Pessimism knocked at the door— faith opened it— and nothing was there." Faith will drive away melancholy.

We need to believe that God has the ability to turn our black storm-clouds into gentle showers of blessing.

This was the faith that kept the early Christians going against the bitterest opposition and gave them power to persevere when it seemed humanly impossible. Faith in God's power to override their adversities propelled them onward with a forward look. This is the explanation found in the Bible: "And we know that all things work together for good to them that love God, to them who are the called according to his purpose" (Romans 8:28).

> *My God, I would not live*
> *Save that I think this gross hard-seeming world*
> *Is our misshaping vision of the Powers*
> *Behind the world that make our griefs our gains.*
> — ALFRED TENNYSON

Faith to accept our burdens as bridges make life's chasms crossable. We can learn from the little ant at our feet. One of them, carrying a straw which seemed too big for it, came to a crevice in the ground. At first the ant, running back and forth, was in a quandary. Finally it pushed the straw across, spanning the crack, and then walked over and picked up the straw and continued the journey. Its burden had become its bridge for progress.

One of the most convincing examples of blessings in disguise is found in the life of Joseph, recorded in the Old Testament. When he was sold by his envious brothers into a life of slavery, it first appeared that his world of greatest usefulness had ended. But it was actually the first step in God's providing a new and larger world of service for him. So Joseph arose from slavery and imprisonment to the second office in all of Egypt, next to Pharaoh himself. As the food administrator, he gathered food to tide them over the seven years of famine. It was God's way of saving His people. Joseph later tearfully explained to those same brothers: "And God sent me before you to preserve you a posterity in the earth, and to save your lives by a great deliverance. So now it was not you that sent me hither, but God" (Genesis 45:7,8).

God had raised up an unknown to a place of rulership for a purpose. The same Father can lift up all who trust and obey. God has the ability to bless us with a richness of life excelling a king, in the things that really count. It is evident from Joseph's life that God can make the nobodies and nothings into kings and queens.

We need to have faith also in ourselves, we have strength which has not been used and power which has not been harnessed. This is true of all of us. Change your mental image of yourself. See yourself as a successful person; and any person who is true to God, to his fellowman and to himself, producing as best he can, regardless of education or occupation, is a success. A college education can be a great help; but without it you can still be an unusual success by fully applying your talents and by believing in yourself. Some of the greatest geniuses were self-educated men and women who conquered their misgivings and learned to believe in their hidden power.

Abraham Lincoln is an illustrious example of optimism.

Even though he kept losing, he believed he could win. The rail-splitter who walked miles for a book and read from the light of an open fireplace refused to be defeated. If he had not believed in himself, he would not have become President. Note the following:

1831— failed in business.
1832— defeated for legislature.
1838— defeated for elector.
1843— defeated for congress.
1848— defeated for senate.
1855— defeated for Vice-President.
1860— elected President of the U.S.

We are repeating the words of the apostle Paul: "I can do all things through Christ which strengtheneth me" (Philippians 4:13). Repeat this statement often. It is an optimist-producer.

• *Another great producer of optimism is the thought, "The memory of the just is blessed"* (Proverbs 10:7). It is not uncommon for justice to be flouted and for evil to be enthroned. The wicked often take advantage of the righteous. There is so much unfairness. But the prosperity of the wicked is only a seeming success. Evil on a throne is still evil and right in a dungeon is still right; and in time their places will be reversed.

Good men in their struggles for right may have been tempted to think as they passed through disappointment's shadows that their labors were in vain. But their warfare has not been for nought. Their heroic stand has made the battles easier for others; and it is in grateful memory of them that we pay tribute to their accomplishments.

Nearly every family has been touched by the death of father, mother, husband, wife, son, daughter, brother or sister. The crepe has hung on the door of almost every home. It will keep on appearing, for time takes its toll. One by one, all will end their earthly pilgrimage. When our loved one passes hence to the "bourn from whence no traveler returns" and we grasp for comfort in our sorrow, it is then that we find a precious ointment to heal our bleeding hearts in a sweet remembrance of what the departed one was, what he stood for, the cause for which he battled, how many stones he removed from the pathway of others, what he meant to us and how much he loved us. These recollections allow the sunshine to break across our pathway.

For the most part, history is on the side of right. Time has a way of correcting wrongs. History usually blesses the just person instead of the glory-seeking faker. No one thinks of Ahab and Nero as he thinks of Moses and Paul. By some standards, all were great; but only the memories of the good are blessed today.

It gives us optimism to keep in mind the glorious truth that "the memory of the just is blessed." It renews out hopes when we live not only for today but for our works which will follow after us when we rest from our labors (Revelation 14:13).

Now when we pause in the midst of what seems to be a lost and hopeless struggle and are tempted to turn back, it is a blessed thing to hear the admonition of some consecrated friend beyond, "Keep up the fight." "He being dead yet speaketh" (Hebrews 11:4). What others are saying by their works, we can say by ours. May God grant us the grace of optimism to leave such a memory.

> *Needs there the praise of the love-written sonnet:*
> *The name and the epitaph graved on the stone?*
> *The things we have lived for, let them be our story,*
> *And we but remembered by what we have done!*

• *Summed up, we can be an optimist by controlling our thoughts.* We will be what we think. The aforementioned principles will guide us in thought-control. We can control our spirit. The Bible says that he who rules his spirit is better than he that takes a city (Proverbs 16:32). There is a greater victory in ruling self than in ruling a city. The control of thoughts, to think optimistically instead of pessimistically, will save us from a thousand imaginary ills. We must take this more realistic view:

> *Though life is made up of mere bubbles*
> *'Tis better than many aver,*
> *For while we've a whole lot of troubles*
> *The most of them never occur.*
> — Nixon Waterman

Flower of Courage

Life is so filled with disappointments and reverses that it takes much courage to keep chasing our dreams. Without it, we would soon slow down to a dull walk.

• *What is courage?* It is an affair of the heart; it is an inward condition which controls outward behavior.

Courage is a streak of bravery running through a person. It is that conquering trait of heroism which enables one to triumph over inward fears and risk fortune and life for a person, a duty or a cause. The soldier who risks his life for his country is applauded as a hero and rightly so. Was he afraid? Yes and no. He sensed danger, grave danger; but he fought his fears and conquered them.

Then there is moral courage, the kind of heroism that often goes unapplauded. The moral victor is called upon to stand for what he believes is right, even though old friends turn against him, cease to know him and slam the door in his face. Many people who have bravely stood against the enemy in carnal war-

fare have not been strong enough to stand against the unrelenting opposition of persecution, ridicule and ostracism. Standing against the crowd calls for a type of bravery which is much too rare.

And there is pluck in everyday living. This is the courage which keeps a person going against all the fear and friction of life's adversities. This is a daily need, because every day has its own problems.

There are family and social entanglements. Unforeseen losses come. Sickness strikes and plays havoc with our plans. Jobs hang in the balance. There are obligations to meet. Reputation is at stake. The children's education must be financed. There are vexatious mistakes, misplaced confidence or hurtful miscalculations. The ties of love are broken by death, and our hearts ache and bleed and break. The demands are great. Pressures build up. It takes courage to bravely bear our burdens and heroically walk through the shadows.

It takes pluck and, someway, somehow the brave come up with it.

Pluck Wins

Pluck wins! It always wins! though days be slow,
And nights be dark 'twixt days that come and go,
Still pluck will win; its average is sure;
He gains the prize who will the most endure;
Who faces issues; he who never shirks;
Who waits and watches, and who always works.

• *God speaks words of courage to His children.* Here are a few of the many courage-giving passages in the Bible:

Be strong and of good courage; be not afraid, neither be thou dismayed: for the Lord thy God is with thee whithersoever thou goest (Joshua 1:9).

Fear thou not; for I am with thee: be not dismayed; for I am thy God: I will strengthen thee: yea, I will help thee; yea, I will uphold thee with the right hand of my righteousness (Isaiah 41:10).

Be strong and of a good courage, fear not, nor be afraid of them: for the Lord thy God, he it is that doth go with thee! he will not fail thee; not forsake thee (Deuteronomy 31:6).

The bravest and strongest have need at times to be recharged with courage. After all, we are human beings. We weaken like a battery; but just as the battery can be recharged with current, we too can be recharged with courage from God's word.

It worked for a man as great as Elijah. This story is found in the Bible (I Kings 19). He felt that the forces of opposition were too strong to combat any longer, that it was a losing fight— "Oh, what's the use?" His morale had dropped too low for struggle; so he fled from Jezebel's threat, from duty and from responsibility. He ran away into the wilderness. Perhaps everyone of us has at times wanted to run away. There he sat down under a tree and requested that he might die.

The Lord, however, dealt tenderly and graciously with Elijah, helping him overcome his fear; for even a prophet is unfitted for the exacting problems of life, if he has become a captive of fear. Then the Lord sent him on his way to complete his work.

All such encouragement is in the Bible for our learning and strength. It is easier to stand our ground when we have something to stand on. It gives us that heroic stuff to become more than we are and to do more than we can.

• *The consciousness of the divine presence of God in our lives gives us bravery and fearlessness.* We are the offspring of God, and as such were not born for a life of fear. As His children, we were created to be afraid of nothing but God and this is the fear that is reverence and awe instead of fright.

God has promised to be with us; so has Jesus who said, "And, lo, I am with you alway, even unto the end of the world" (Matthew 28:20). One of our faults is that we have taken these words only as a vague promise. We have failed to translate this truth into an absolute and real promise that protects us from beginning to end. But as soon as the believer comes to see that this promise stands for a precious reality, he will receive an added strength that makes heroes out of otherwise weak human beings.

This consciousness of God will give us the experience of courage as recorded in the reassuring language of others who found this extra bravery:

We are troubled; we are perplexed, but not in despair; persecuted, but not forsaken; cast down, but not destroyed (II Corinthians 4:8,9).

Nay, in all these things we are more than conquerors through him that loved us (Romans 8:37).

An awareness of God's presence gives us a strength stronger than ourselves to face adversities. Though we are hit hard and often by an opposing world, we never can be beaten down— that is, to stay down, for we will rise to face another day that is more favorable.

It is this assurance which gives us the kind of courage to face death. Many of the early Christians were executed in wholesale lots by the cruelest means. They went to the crosses, to the pots of boiling oil and to the lions in the arena without a murmur of fear. One of the heathen rulers commented, "There is one thing you can say about those Christians: they know how to die."

A superhuman courage born of a power greater than themselves made them "more than conquerors."

Cares may await you— dangers may pursue,
Grief melt the heart, and sickness cloud the view—
But God is with you; His strong arm shall be
A tower of strength in your adversity—
A present help your fainting hearts to cheer—
Your staff and comfort in the night of fear!
— POLYNESIA

• *The hope of immortality gives us courage.* Hope is spoken of as "an anchor of the soul, both sure and steadfast" (Hebrews 6:19). It keeps us from being helplessly tossed on the stormy waves of fear. With hope of another life we are not fearful of today's battle, because our real future is not tied in with time but with eternity. It makes a great difference when we have the hope that it is not all of life to live nor all of death to die. Many a person would have long since fainted in life's struggle without the inward strength of hope. The Bible says:

> For which cause we faint not; but though our outward man perish, yet the inward man is renewed day by day.
>
> For our light affliction, which is but for a moment, worketh for us a far more exceeding and eternal weight of glory;
>
> While we look not at the things which are seen; but at the things which are not seen: for the things which are seen are temporal; but the things which are not seen are eternal.
>
> —II CORINTHIANS 4:16-18

If fear is one of our most paralyzing weaknesses, then courage is one of our most powerful forces. We need the courage of Alexander the Great. His soldiers told him that there were so many Persians that "when they draw their bows, their arrows will be so numerous that they willl darken the sun."

The Emperor replied, "In that case, it will be so fine to fight in the shade." No wonder the world calls him great.

Flower of Perseverance

O ne of our greatest needs is the old tough and rugged quality of perseverance; because one of our greatest temptations is instability, a wavering, a turning aside.

We need to remember that God has no pleasure in the quitter. "If any man draw back, my soul shall have no pleasure in him" (Hebrews 10:38).

Be sure you are right and go ahead. "Hold fast that which is good" (I Thessalonians 5:21).

"If thou faint in the day of adversity, thy strength is small" (Proverbs 24:10).

• *Persistence is essential to success in every walk of life.* It is the one neck ahead that wins the race; it is the one pull more on the oars that puts one in front; it is the one march more that gives an army the strategic position in battle; it is the one hour more of persistent courage that wins the fight. Though our strength be less than another's we outmaster our opponent if we continue longer and concentrate more. The reply of the gen-

eral to his soldier who complained that his sword was too short, "Add a step to it," is applicable to all of us in every duty of life.

We have literally used enough keys trying to unlock a door to know the value of perseverance. We have learned to keep trying, for it is usually the last key on the ring that fits the lock.

The Founding Fathers understood the necessity of enduring hardships. They knew they could not quench their thirst from the sparkling spring nor eat of the hidden honey, if they were annoyed by briars and bee stings. We have moved out of the wilderness— one kind— and into a different manner of earning a living, but the need for perseverance has not lessened. Today it is not the briars and the bees, but it is bills and bills, which necessitate work and work.

Every age has its problems and every heart has its sorrows. But neither the problems can be solved nor the sorrows healed by giving up. God expects us to continue the race until it is over and victory is won.

• *But whether we go on or drop in our tracks will be largely determined by our thoughts.* We become the creatures of our own thinking. The Bible says, "For as he thinketh in his heart, so is he" (Proverbs 23:7). Whether we become quitters or victors will be determined by the thoughts in the heart. How important it is then that we think victoriously. Tell yourself that you can fight your battles, that you can bear your burdens, that you can solve your problems, that you can meet your obligations, that you can endure your suffering, that you can succeed, that you can rise above adversities, that you can be happy where you are. A sea of angry circumstances can drown us or we can ride the waves to new shores.

A few days ago we were reading the story of a great and ancient man whose name was Epictetus. He was born about 50 A.D. into a biting, snarling world of very poor, heathen parents. His parents were so poor that in keeping with heathen practice, they sold him into slavery. Furthermore, he was deformed and sickly. Epictetus was taken to Rome where he was owned by the secretary or librarian of the cruel and infamous Nero who placed him among his numerous slaves and put him to work at the most menial tasks.

What chance did a deformed slave-boy have? The answer to the question was found inside the boy. What did he have there? What were his thoughts? It is the inside of man that counts the most. It is the inside that causes some to succeed and others to fail, some to be courageous and others fearful. This maimed slave with extraordinary internal fortitude arose above his handicaps and became one of the world's great teachers, and his words still teach. Here are two of his insightful statements:

For no one is a slave whose will is free.
What ought not to be done do not think of doing.

Motivated by a noble self-respect, though Epictetus was externally nothing but a lame slave, he glorified his slavery. He made the low and degrading confines of servitude something far above the common and menial task. The control of his thoughts which produced self-discipline, self-courage, self-determination and high motivation lifted him up. The same thing can make our own poor plight and leaden tasks, whatever they are, take on a new meaning. The secret is in right thinking. As Epictetus said, "What ought not to be done do not think of doing." Whatever our burden is, we can never bear it by fainting beneath it; so never think of quitting.

• *Perseverance requires a definite decision backed up by an iron will.* This is seen from this Scripture: " They went forth to go into the land of Canaan; and into the land of Canaan they came" (Genesis 12:5).

The passage states two conditions for success in life. The first is decision, meaning that we must decide upon the right goal for which to start in life— "They went forth to go into the land of Canaan." The second is perseverance, meaning that we must keep on going after we have started— "Into the land of Canaan they came."

A friend who quit a bad habit explained that it was easy when he once made up his mind to quit. The power of decision is a dynamic force.

Suppose we had to face the strain and static, wear and tear, of these trials and tribulations:

In labors more abundant, in stripes above measure, in prisons more frequent, in deaths oft. Of the
Jews five times received I forty strips save one. Thrice
was I beaten with rods, once was I stoned, thrice I suf-

fered shipwreck, a night and a day I have been in the
deep; in journeyings often, in perils of waters, in perils
of robbers, in perils by mine own countrymen, in peril
by heathen, in peril in the city, in perils in the wilderness, in perils in the sea, in perils among false brethren;
in weariness and painfulness, in watchings often, in
hunger and thirst, in fastings often, in cold and naked-
ness. Beside those things that are without, that which
cometh upon me daily, the care of all the churches.

— II Corinthians 11:23-28

Did a man actually stand up against all these hardships?
Yes! An excellent Christian by the name of Paul. Those troubles
came upon him because he dared to preach Christ. He was
finally beheaded outside the city of Rome, and shortly before
death he wrote, "I have fought a good fight, I have finished my
course, I have kept the faith" (II Timothy 4:7). He met road-
blocks but kept going. He was rebuffed but undefeated. He was
martyred but unconquered. A thousand voices in amazement
ask, "How could he do it?" He had made a decision, a decision
for Christ and for truth and for right, and he supported it with
an unconquerable will. He lived for a purpose.

• *Power of purpose lends energy and fight for the struggle.*

A visitor to a large southwestern ranch once made the following observation:

"One morning I watched a couple of cow punchers going
out to bring in a wild steer from the range in certain mountains.

They took along one of those shaggy little gray donkeys, a burro.

"Now a big three year old steer that's been running loose in the timber is a tough customer to handle. Those cowboys had the technique. They got a rope on the steer; then they tied him to the burro, neck and neck right up close. When they let go, that burro had a bad time. The steer threw him all over the place. He banged him against trees, rocks, in the bushes. But there was one great difference between the burro and the steer. The burro had an idea. He wanted to go home. And no matter how often the steer threw him, every time the burro got to his feet he took a step nearer the corral. This went on and on. After about a week the burro showed up at ranch headquarters. He had with him the tamest and sorriest looking steer you ever saw."

The moral is that no amount of beef, brains or education will suffice where worthwhile purpose is lacking.

What that burro lacked in size and weight he overcame by purpose which gave direction to his movements and kept him at it.

• *Without thinking of looking back, the fixed heart keeps us looking ahead.* The Psalmist said, "O God, my heart is fixed" (Psalm 108:1). This is an example of the decision, iron will and power of purpose of which we have spoken— and it comes from the inside.

Solomon said, "Let thine eyes look right on, and let thine eyelids look straight before thee" (Proverbs 4:25). Men and women often lose in their struggle against poverty, ignorance, spiritual darkness and sometimes poor health because they take their eyes off the goal. The heart was not securely fixed. They would like to have the blessings which come from a fixed purpose— financial security, education, good reputation, friends and heaven's smiles— but they are unwilling to pay the price. The burdens seem too heavy and the way up looks too steep and far, but remember there are no elevators in the house of success. We must work our way up a step at a time or stay where we are.

• *As we grapple with our difficulties and triumph over them, we become stronger.* Too much easy living makes us like a mushroom, which grows up in a night but is only a pulpy thing. The oak— ah, there is something solid, and there are people who persevere like the oak. "And he shall be like a tree planted by the rivers of water" (Psalm 1:3). The winds howl with the threat, "We will break you"; but the oak stretches out its strong limbs and answers, "Let's see you try it." The rocks midst the roots grindingly mutter, "We'll stop you"; but the oak wrestles with the rocks, conquers them, and sends its roots down deeper. Thus like the oak, we have to persevere and wrestle for the graces we call character. Discouragement? At times. Blunder? Often. Give up? No! Never!

When difficulty develops, greet it with determination. When danger arises, meet it with courage. You will be strengthened for new tasks. On thy way. Straight ahead.

Sweet are the uses of adversity;
Which, like the toad, ugly and venomous,
Wears yet a precious jewel in his head;
And this our life, exempt from public haunt,
Finds tongues in trees, books in the running brooks,
Sermons in stones, and good in everything.

— WILLIAM SHAKESPEARE

• *Those who persevere must fight discouragement.* Encouragement is courage within and it can be lost. Gloom can develop from disenchantment, a sense of inexplorable weariness and a sense of inevitable disappointment. Discouragement has defeated many who had the other necessary attributes to succeed.

When you feel discouraged, look for good and listen for good news. We usually find that for which we look.

If you are tempted to give up in the struggle for right, believing the world is going to the dogs anyway, just remember that you can turn the dogs away and stop the growth of evil by standing for the right. Just one person with God on his side constitutes an immeasurable power.

If you feel dismayed because your life seems so insignificant and what you do looks so little, bear in mind there are no earthly gauges to determine whether a life or an act is little or big. With God, some of the things that seem little are big, and some of the things that seem big are little. In keeping with this principle, Jesus stated that the widow who gave two mites had given more than all the big contributors. It was the best she could do— that is what counts.

Find out what God would have you do,
And do that little well;
For what is great and what is small
'Tis only he can tell.

So here is a vigorous resolution of encouragement and perseverance for every one of us:

I am only one;
But, I am one.
I cannot do everything;
But, I can do something.
What I can do, I ought to do:
And what I ought to do,
By the grace of God,
I will do.

Flower of Staying Young

he buoyancy of youth is a good gift of God. Young hearts are filled with faith, hope, love, ambition and resolve.

So nigh is grandeur to our dust,
So near is God to man,
When duty whispers low, "Thou must,"
The Youth replies, "I can."

Courage puts a twinkle in the eye and a smile in the cheek. To youth the coming of a new day is a thrilling experience. They know neither the limits of their abilities nor the dangers ahead. They travel the journey of life with a reserve of freshness and vigor. Every day is like the growing of a beautiful flower. Of course, there are some problems and anxieties for youth— just like the rose blossoms amidst the thorns— but they are insignificant in comparison with the joy of youthful living, just like the

thorns are as nothing in comparison with the beauty and fragrance of the rose.

Fortunately some people stay perpetually young, not in body but in spirit, not the outward man but the inward man. Of all the personal accomplishments, this is one of the most rewarding. This is what everybody prefers but only a few achieve. In speaking of staying internally young while the years slip away, the Bible says, "But though our outward man perish, yet the inward man is renewed day by day" (II Corinthians 4:16).

Whatever our chronological age may be, here are some suggestions to keep us young:

• *The factor which really determines our youthful personality is not our years but our heart.* This is seen from the above-quoted passage in the Bible. Thus youth cannot be confined to those with few years, few sorrows and few problems; but it rather includes those who are young in heart. They are the ones who keep on believing, hoping, loving and looking forward. They have no gnawing hate, frustrating resentment, biting vengeance or disturbing doubts to make them old on the inside. With a faith akin to that of a child, every new day is to them like the joys of childhood all over again. They look to every day for life.

Look To This Day

Look to this day, for it is life; the very life of life. In its brief course lie all the verities and realities of your existence; the bliss of growth, the glory of action, the splendor of beauty. For yesterday is but a dream, and tomorrow is only a

*vision; but today, well lived, makes every yesterday a dream
of happiness and every tomorrow a vision of hope. Look
well, therefore, to this day. Such is the salutation of the
dawn.*

— FROM THE SANSCRIT

Oh, yes, these young people with many birthdays have had
their share of adversities just like the rest of us have had. The
difference is in their reaction to them. The same fire which
hardens the clay melts the tallow; and they, like the tallow, have
been softened and mellowed by the fiery experiences of life.

The young in heart have known pain, disappointment, misplaced confidence, weakness, calamity, sadness and bereavement.
The clouds have hovered over them. They have walked into shadows. They have heard life's thunder in their noonday. They have
seen their sun of expectations grow dark as it went down behind
the storm clouds. They have seen their circle of earthly friends
grow smaller and smaller. They themselves have at times walked
close to the brink of the valley of the shadow of death.

Yet life continues to be so pleasant and meaningful that
they feel the world is their friend. Even though they have
passed many milestones in the journey of life, they have become
neither weary nor footsore in the march. They are carrying their
old burdens of duty, care and sorrow with a daily renewal of
zest and vigor. As their bodies become older, their spirits
become younger.

• *We can retain youth by thinking like a young person.* We

become the product of our thinking. The Bible says, "For as he thinketh in his heart, so is he" (Proverbs 23:7). All of us understand that physical strength must give way to the years, but internally a person is only as old as he thinks. Unfortunately many people in their later years have allowed their thinking to give them calendar neurosis. This is the dread of turning the calendar. It is the killing idea that one is getting old and his usefulness is waning. This kind of thinking makes one old quickly, increases morbid anxiety and adds to one's helplessness.

• *Stay young by taking time to live.* From the physical viewpoint we are dying a little every day we pass the brink of the grave, and some of its dust is sprinkled upon us. But we can shake off some dust for awhile by taking time to enjoy the deeper and more meaningful things of life. It is true that we must make a living; but as we do, let us not forget to live a life. Not only do the cares of the world choke the word of God in our hearts (Matthew 13:22), but they also choke youth and wreck health.

A doctor told the story of a patient who was getting old in middle age. The patient thought his business could not go on without him; so he worked overtime night after night, and would take a brief case full of work home with him on the weekend. His explanation to the physician was that the work had to be done and that he was the only one who could do it. The pressure was killing him.

The doctor refused to prescribe until the patient agreed to follow the prescription, which was this: He was to deliberately cut off two hours of every working day and spend that time cultivating traits and attitudes which keep one young. He was to take off a half day every week and spend the time in a cemetery. The doctor said, "I want you to wander around and look at the gravestones of those who thought the whole world rested on their shoulders and who had no time to enjoy the finer aspects of life. And then meditate on the fact that when you are rolled there to lie in hallowed soil, the world will keep on turning and it will be found that you were not so indispensable after all. Then sit down among the tombstones and quote two verses from the Bible: 'Boast not thyself of tomorrow; for thou knowest not what a day may bring forth' (Proverbs 27:1). 'A merry heart doeth good like a medicine: but a broken spirit drieth the bones' (Proverbs 27:22)."

In a few weeks the patient got better and recovered some of the invigorating qualities of youth he was losing. His business improved. His change was so marked that his friends and business associates liked him better and appreciated his company more.

Gather ye rose-buds while ye may,
Old time is still flying,
And this same flower that smiles today,
Tomorrow will be dying.

• *The ability to see the unseen keeps us young.* The secret strength of Moses which gave him the youthful courage to stand against the strongest opposition was his ability to see beyond this world of hardships and sorrows and catch a vision of the invisible. The Bible gives this explanation and pays this tribute to this brave man who was one of the greatest leaders of all times: "For he endured, as seeing him who is invisible" (Hebrews 11:27). With him, age was no problem because his eyes were not on self but on the invisible. His mind was not on self and the multiplication of his years, but on a cause and the multiplication of its greatness. Moses could see what many others could not see. It kept him persevering in trials, believing in defeats, hopeful in sorrow and courageous in conflict— summed up, it kept him young in heart. He had something to live for, because he had something to live with— the dedication to a great cause.

Moses was eighty years of age when God called him to lead Israel out of bondage, and although Moses first asked to be excused because his verbal skills were not good, it is encouraging to all of us to note that he did not ask to be excused from this rigorous task on account of his age (Exodus 4:10). Moses did not have an old age complex.

Life becomes stale and boresome to those who can see no further than self-interests, self-cares and self-gratifications. When they have selfishly exhausted all the springs of material enjoyment, when they have gulped down the last dregs of self-gratification until there is little left to be gratified, then there is no wonder that their days are full of anxiety, fretfulness and weariness. It makes them psychologically old regardless of their years.

• *We can keep ourselves young by welcoming the aids and ministries of life.* The words of a well known hymn, sung in the house of worship, will lift up our drooping spirits and put new life in our sagging steps. The voice of a good man, speaking from the Holy Bible, will send us along the pathway of life with fresh energy and new resolve.

The performance of a good deed every day adds interest to life and keeps our days from being just an aging process of eating, drinking and sleeping in an animal existence.

Working with the Boy Scouts of Girl Scouts, engaging in civic improvements, teaching a Bible class at church, rendering aid in the church's benevolent program, will add a new spark to our years.

Then there is a renewal of life in reading. Many an invalid child and many an elderly person, sick in body, could tell us hour after hour what their books have done to brighten their outlook on life.

• *The sparkle of youth may be retained by the happy associations and hopeful voices of our sons and daughters and grandchildren.* One grand preventive of heart-weariness which makes one old is the loving contact with the lives of others. Love is a wonderful freshener of human life. Love manifests itself by seeking the welfare of those that are loved. The Bible says that love seeks not her own, endures all things and never fails (I Corinthians 13). So long as we keep on really living, life can never lose its usefulness; and so long as we are helpful in at least some capacity— economic, physical, mental, moral or spiritual— life can never lose its zest. There is a youthful freshness in all genuine, unselfish affection.

We have seen new grandparents brighten up and become twenty years younger because of the coming of the grandchild. The grandbaby gave them a new interest in life. One grandfather explained it this way: "I feel younger than ever because I have so much more to live for. I am making new plans. That baby has given me a new lease on life."

All of us, whether we have children or not, will help ourselves by linking our lives in sympathy and service with lives that are younger than our own. People with many birthdays, who have begun to feel that life has lost its meaning, can be revived and cheered by the glad touch of some little child, as by the touch of an angel's hand. "It is more blessed to give than to receive" (Acts 20:35).

The Never-Old

They who can smile when others hate
Nor bind the heart with frosts of fate,
Their feet will go with laughter bold
The green roads of the Never-Old.

They who can let the spirit shine
And keep the heart a lighted shrine,
Their feet will glide with fire-of-gold
The bright roads of the Never-Old.

They who can put the self aside
And in Love's saddle leap and ride,
Their eyes will see the gates unfold
To glad roads of the Never-Old.

— EDWIN MARKHAM

Flower of Solitude

A n evangelist preaching in a city for two weeks was rushed unnecessarily with too many engagements. He was hurried to several meetings during the day. Toward the close of his stay they rushed him to his hotel room with an urgent admonition to get ready fast, for he had just twenty minutes to dress for dinner. At the meeting, as usual, he was scheduled to make a speech. As he was dressing, the telephone rang and someone said, "Hurry! Hurry! We are ready to eat." He said that he would be there in a minute. As he stepped outside the room he was so nervous he could hardly lock the door. Then he hastened down the hall to the elevator, all out of breath. Before he got on, however, he rationally said to himself, "What am I doing! I don't care whether I go to this dinner or not; I'm not really hungry. I don't care whether I make this speech or not; I have more important speeches to make." He turned around and went to his room, locked the door, telephoned the man in charge and said "Go ahead and eat. I don't want to

delay you. If you want to save a place for me, then save it; and I will be down after awhile." Then he took off his coat, loosened his tie, sat in a chair, put his feet on the table and began to meditate in solitude. He opened his Bible and read three passages:

> Be silent, O all flesh, before the Lord: for he is raised up out of his holy habitation.
>
> — ZECHARIAH 2:13

> But the Lord is in his holy temple: let all the earth keep silence before him.
>
> —HABAKKUK 2:20

> I will lift up mine eyes unto the hills, from whence cometh my help. My help cometh from the Lord, which made heaven and earth...The Lord shall preserve thy going out and thy coming in from this time forth, and even for evermore.
>
> —PSALM 121

Then he began to hum and meditate on a portion of the grand old hymn, *Take Time to Be Holy:*

> *Take time to be holy, the world rushes on;*
> *Spend much time in secret with Jesus alone;*
> *By looking to Jesus, like him thou shalt be;*
> *Thy friends in thy conduct His likeness shall see.*

Take time to be holy, be calm in thy soul;
Each tho't and each motive beneath his control;
Thus led by His Spirit to fountains of love,
Thou soon shalt be fitted for service above.

Next he prayed a little prayer: "O God, keep my nerves from becoming tattered from the little conventionalities of our society, that they may be as strong as iron for the big issues of life. Keep me from becoming footsore in a mad race that leads almost nowhere, that I may have the readiness to take the steps that really count. In Christ's name. Amen"

Then as he sat there and meditated he said to himself. "Relax. God is here. If I am quiet now, I will make a better speech later." He sat there for fifteen minutes, calmly walked out of the room a different man, in complete control of himself. He went down to the banquet, and about all he had missed was a little bowl of soup.

• *We have reached the point where we can make better time by slowing down.* Truly this is an age out of breath, broken-winded, hurrying to the grave at a terrific speed. We are living hard, restless, mechanical lives. We have very little time for rest, retreat and seclusion. In shifting to high gear, our civilization has pulled away from quietude, tranquility and contentment. To regain what we have left behind, several things are necessary, one of which is to slow down.

• *We have imprisoned ourselves.* A peculiar jail cell describes our society. It is a revolving cage. The prisoner who is suspected of trying to break out is placed in this cell which is kept moving, revolving all the time. He is not permitted to stay in one place long enough to dig out at the sides. Many people in riding their materialistic merry-go-round are actual prisoners in their own revolving cell. They need to stop the mad rush of life and break out of the prison of their own making. Solitude with its quiet reflection and deep meditation can free man from the throbbing tumult which stifles the growth of his soul and mind.

> *Stone walls do not a prison make,*
> *Nor iron bars a cage;*
> *Minds innocent and quiet take*
> *That for a hermitage;*
> *If I have freedom in my love,*
> *And in my soul am free*
> *Angles alone, that soar above,*
> *Enjoy such liberty*
> —RICHARD LOVELACE

• *Our new vain society is cheating us out of the rest and solitude we once enjoyed.* The results have been less rejuvenation and peace, more ulcers and breakdowns. Much thought is given to making a living, but only a little thought is given to living a life. Consequently we are too fatigued to enjoy the higher values.

A weary father said, "I am so tired, but that is not strange for I have not felt rested in ten years." He was toiling hard; his responsibilities were heavy; and the strain was showing in his face and in his steps. His expenses were extra heavy: a costly house, increased utilities, two automobiles, delicious food, good clothes, high taxes, insurance payments, extra help in the house and the children's education. Most of the time he worked seven days a week, and seldom ever was his mind free of pressing obligations during his waking hours. In anticipation of a new day, however, he brightened up and said, "I figure in another five years I can take life a little easier."

All noble people appreciate his unselfish industry and devotion to his family's happiness and security. But a bit more common sense and a little more thoughtfulness on his part, and maybe on the part of others in the family would have made that anticipated rest in tomorrow's uncertainty today's reality. They could have more joy on less expense, for what appears to make for peace of mind seldom does. Happiness has a way of fleeing from those who try to buy it. The reason is it comes free. One of the requirements, however, is that we take time to enjoy life.

• *Much of our unrest today can be charged to our speeding through life.* We seem to be running downhill and the farther we go the faster we must run to keep from falling, but the speed becomes too great and in time we spill. We are pursued day and night by the demon hurry. We become exhausted, irritable, and the sparks of friction may fly. We are sucked dry as a squeezed lemon and almost as sour. The greater tragedy is that we get up early the next morning to repeat the same slavish routine.

• *Solitude is essential because it is in the inner chamber of the soul that we find and enjoy the most satisfying rest.* It is there that we see the unlimited power of God controlling all things, His unerring wisdom guiding the affairs of the universe, His unblemished love and pity yearning for all people, His unfailing light illuminating the darkness and His unmarred righteousness eventually triumphing — this is rest. To put off the galling weight of cares from our shoulders that God may carry them for us — soul troubles, home cares, business worries, national problems and fears for the future — this is rest. To be freed from the bitterness and turmoil of a troubled world, to find refuge in God, to feel that His everlasting arms are underneath us — this is rest, deep and unutterable rest for the soul, "the peace of God, which passeth all understanding" (Philippians 4:7).

• *Solitude was one of the strengthening experiences in the life of Jesus.* He often left the multitudes that He might retreat to some quiet solitary place. This is especially seen in the last week of His earthly life in the flesh. As events reached the climax, He needed all His strength and fortitude to fulfill His mission.

On Sunday of the last week he made His triumphal entry into Jerusalem amidst an exciting and tumultuous welcome in which the people spread their garments and tree branches before Him and shouted: "Hosanna; Blessed is he that cometh in the name of the Lord." But Jesus knew the fickleness of man — those same people, as putty in the hands of self-seeking leaders, a few days later were shouting, "Let him be crucified." After visiting the temple "And when he had looked round about upon all things, and now the eventide was come, he went out unto Bethany with the twelve" (Mark 11:11).

The twilight hour has always been the choice time for weary and burdened souls to meditate. It catches us between a day spent and a night emerging. It is there that we stand between the shadowy East and the fiery West and fast falls the eventide with its night descending.

The journey to Bethany was a beautiful and restful one. As Jesus walked that road, free from the multitude's noise and bickering strife, saw the golden sunset fading among the distant hills, beheld the rising silvery moon gliding over the olive trees and inhaled the fragrance of a thousand flowers, He surely felt the recreating power of nature and of God.

On Monday morning He went back to Jerusalem for there was more work to be done, but "When even was come" He returned to the quiet of Bethany.

On Tuesday morning He again re-entered the worldly and busy Jerusalem, but as night approached He retired to Bethany.

Jesus then spent Wednesday and the greater portion of Thursday in absolute retirement from the world. Little is known of this pause in His life. It is called the silent period. The Master evidently used the silence to fortify Himself against the chilling shadows that would soon fall across His path, blot out the sun and envelop the land in darkness for three hours (Mark 15:33). He knew the end was near. We are persuaded this silent period among His own was a time of deep serenity and golden peace. It prepared Him for the fearful struggle.

It is evident that Jesus preferred the calm and tranquility of the country to the noises and turbulence of the city. He loved the solitude of the mountains, the breathless colors that tint the peaceful hills and the aroma of the freshened air on the heights. How invigorating must have been those evening walks amid the twilight where angry voices had died away and where nature was at rest. How exhilarating must have been that silent pause in His life which afforded the the closest touch with God and friends, free from distractions.

Christ's example is a lesson for all of us. For everyone of us there are voices of strength to be heard out of the solemn stillness. There are the meditations, thoughts which go deeper than we have ever experienced, the determined resolutions, and the mustering of strength from an inner being braver and stronger than we thought we possessed. As a result we become as courageous as a lion and as harmless as a kitten, as determined as a brave soldier and as restful as a cradled child.

When a heavy sorrow bleeds our heart, or a vexing problem crushes our soul, and the hurt is so deep we are unable to measure its depth, it is then that silence is golden and solitude is strengthening. We whisper to the crowd, "Just let me be alone for awhile and I think I shall be all right." It is in the solitude that we search our soul and come to know ourselves better.

We have sat with sorely troubled friends for rather long periods in which neither uttered a word. It seemed better to say nothing at the time, for words would keep. But the silence was a soothing balm for broken hearts. How often have we attempted to speak comforting words to the distressed sick, or to the anguished bereaved bent over their departed loved ones, only to find it more helpful to say nothing at the moment. For them to know that we were near, plus the power of silence, did more for them than our words could do.

Lest we be misunderstood, we hasten to say that under most circumstances we need to speak. The person with a message needs to be heard, but must know when to say it. There are times when we should:

Hold with each, in unvoiced sympathy,
The sweet commune of friends, and come to know
The golden speech of silence.

The saddest thing about the rush of our materialistic days is that they rob us of our silence and communion with God. Silence permits us to think and as we think we are. Inner greatness is no more possible without prayer and communion with God than life is without food.

Then on Friday of that historic week in which never before was death so deathless, goodness so good, purity so pure, and mercy so merciful, several hours before dawn, Jesus took the apostles and went into the Garden of Gethsemane. Stationing the others behind, He took Peter, James and John and went farther into the garden. But feeling the need of more solitude He asked them to tarry behind while He alone went deeper into the garden. There He fell upon His face and prayed.

If Jesus, the Son of God, needed to retire from society's competition and crushing grind to have some solitude in preparation for the coming crisis, then how much more necessary it is for us poor, feeble mortals to break away every day from life's cares for a few moments of silence.

Christ said, "But then, when thou prayest, enter into thy closet, and when thou hast shut thy door, pray to thy Father which is in secret; and thy Father which seeth in secret shall reward thee openly" (Matthew 6:6).

The closet, the lonely place, provides an opportunity for both solitude and prayer. Our well-being requires both.

By all means use some times to be alone.
Salute thyself; see what thy soul doth wear.
       —GEORGE HERBERT